SOJOURNER TRUTH · MADELEINE L'ENGLE
POCAHONTAS · ELIZABETH BLACKWELL
WILMA RUDOLPH · KATHARINA VON BORA
NARCISSA WHITMAN · ELISABETH ELLIOT
KATHERINE G. JOHNSON · JEANETTE LI
JOAN OF ARC · FLANNERY O'CONNOR
CLARA BARTON · SUSAN B. ANTHONY
JONI EARECKSON TADA · NANCY PEARCEY
CONDOLEEZZA RICE · MOTHER TERESA
BETTY OLSEN · HARRIET BEECHER STOWE
FLORENCE NIGHTINGALE · JANE AUSTEN
CORAZON AQUINO · JENNIFER WISEMAN
MARY STONE (SHI METYU) · IDA LEWIS

PANDITA RAMABAI · CHRISTINE CAINE
ROSA PARKS · BETHANY HAMILTON
RUBY BRIDGES HALL · HANNAH
MORE · GABRIELLE "GABBY" DOUGLAS
AMANDA SMITH · HARRIET ROSS TUBMAN
MAHALIA JACKSON · AMY CARMICHAEL
NI KWEI-TSENG SOONG · LYDIA DARRAGH
SABINA WURMBRAND · DOROTHY DAY
CORNELIA "CORRIE" TEN BOOM · PHILLIS
WHEATLEY · TAMIKA CATCHINGS SMITH
JOSEPHINE BUTLER · CATHERINE BOOTH
ANNE BRADSTREET · ELIZABETH GREEN
CATHERINE of SIENA · FANNY CROSBY

Courageous WORLD CHANGERS

by SHIRLEY RAYE REDMOND

ILLUSTRATIONS BY Katya Longhi

HARVEST HOUSE PUBLISHERS
EUGENE, OREGON

Scripture quotations are taken from the Holy Bible, New International Version®, NIV®. Copyright © 1973, 1978, 1984, 2011 by Biblica, Inc.® Used by permission. All rights reserved worldwide.

Cover design by Juicebox Designs

Interior design by KUHN Design Group

Published in association with Books & Such Literary Management, 52 Mission Circle, Suite 122, PMB 170, Santa Rosa, CA 954095370, www.booksandsuch.com.

HARVEST KIDS is a trademark of The Hawkins Children's LLC. Harvest House Publishers, Inc., is the exclusive licensee of the trademark HARVEST KIDS.

Courageous World Changers
Text copyright © 2020 by Shirley Raye Redmond
Illustrations copyright © 2020 by Harvest House Publishers

Published by Harvest House Publishers
Eugene, Oregon 97408
www.harvesthousepublishers.com

ISBN 978-0-7369-7734-0 (hardcover)

Library of Congress CataloginginPublication Data is on file at the Library of Congress, Washington, DC.

Printed in China

21 22 23 24 25 26 27 / RP / 10 9 8 7 6

Contents

Introduction

Faithful Christian women are like salt and light in their communities. They all make a difference. But some have such a vibrant faith that—like a stone tossed into a pond—their influence ripples throughout the world. The fifty women included in this book fall into that category. Each took seriously Jesus's words in Matthew 28:18: "All authority in heaven and on earth has been given to me."

Blessed with a variety of talents—writing and preaching, teaching and nursing—these women used their gifts to glorify God. Aviators and athletes, musicians and mathematicians, many of them forged their faith in the fires of persecution, prejudice, and pain.

Several entered the mission field. Others took their faith into the world of politics or medicine. Strong, smart, and sometimes outspoken, they recognized Jesus as Lord of everything, including the arts and sciences, education, and athletics.

These brief cameos of strong women will inspire young girls to live out their own Christian faith in bold and innovative ways. As the courageous reformer Pandita Ramabai once declared, "A life committed to Christ has nothing to fear, nothing to lose, and nothing to regret."[1]

Cornelia "Corrie" ten Boom
Dutch Underground Volunteer

{ 1892–1983 }

Corrie ten Boom was the youngest of four children in a Dutch family known for their Christian zeal. They invited soldiers, servant girls, and children with mental disabilities to their home for meals, prayer, and Bible study. Corrie helped her mother in the kitchen and her father in his watch shop. After special training in Switzerland, Corrie became the first woman in the Netherlands to become a licensed watchmaker.

During World War II, Corrie became the organizer of a secret ring of eighty Dutch volunteers who helped Jews escape the Holocaust. She and her sister Betsie designed a special hiding place inside their home. They also developed a secret code to deliver messages safely.

One day, betrayed by an informant, Corrie and her family were arrested by the German secret police. They were handcuffed, beaten, and sent to a deplorable concentration camp in Germany, where they lived with meager food, overflowing toilets, and biting fleas. Corrie smuggled a Bible inside her dress. It was never discovered even though she was searched many times. After nearly a year, Betsie died. Corrie was heartbroken, but she was eventually freed to return to Holland.

She wrote about her experiences in a popular book titled *The Hiding Place*. Corrie traveled to more than sixty countries, sharing the good news about Jesus and forgiveness. She said, "Never be afraid to trust an unknown future to a known God."[2]

Corrie died peacefully on her ninety-first birthday, surrounded by friends and birthday bouquets from well-wishers around the world.

Cornelia "Corrie" ten Boom

Pandita Ramabai
Social Reformer

{ 1858–1922 }

Pandita Ramabai's father, a Sanskrit scholar, trained his daughter rigorously in the art of memorization. By the time she was twenty, Pandita spoke five languages and could recite 18,000 verses of the Hindu holy book. After her parents starved during a famine, Pandita traveled to Calcutta. There she became an overnight sensation as a female scholar, which was unheard of at the time.

Moved by compassion for the plight of millions of childhood widows—some as young as eight years old—Pandita dedicated her life to social reform. In 1889, she became the first woman to address the National Social Congress in Bombay, pleading boldly on behalf of the girls starving on the streets or exploited as temple slaves.

Although Hindu scholars rejected her when she converted to Christianity, Pandita testified, "I realized after reading the fourth chapter of St. John's Gospel that Christ was truly the Divine Savior he claimed to be, and no one but he could transform and uplift the downtrodden women of India."[3]

Pandita was a born leader, trusted by the poor and respected by the rich. A lively speaker who moved her audience to tears and laughter, Pandita lectured in India, Great Britain, and the United States. Her fundraising efforts allowed her to open the Mukti Mission School in India. Traveling in disguise, she rescued destitute girls and widows, piling them into an oxcart to transport them to her school.

Despite her busy schedule, Pandita still found time to translate the Bible into her native Marathi language before she died.

Pandita Ramabai

Elizabeth Greene
Missionary Pilot

{ 1920–1997 }

Elizabeth Greene was the first pilot to fly for the Mission Aviation Fellowship.

As a little girl, Betty was fascinated by airplanes. She eagerly read news stories about Amelia Earhart and Charles Lindbergh. Betty saved her pennies, and at the age of sixteen, she began flight lessons. She dreamed of a life of travel and adventure.

Before her dream could come true, the United States became embroiled in World War II. Betty joined the Women Airforce Service Pilots. She flew radar missions and even piloted B-17 bombers in high-altitude equipment tests.

After the war, one of her friends suggested that she become a missionary pilot. Betty admitted, "My mind leaped for joy at the thrilling thought of combining flying with my love for God."[4]

When former Navy pilot Jim Truxton learned about Betty's interest in mission aviation, he wrote to her, suggesting they form an organization of Christian pilots. Soon Betty was helping missionaries all around the world. She flew supplies to missionaries in Mexico and Peru. She became the first woman to pilot an airplane over the Andes Mountains in South America. She flew over deserts and jungles in Africa. She delivered medical supplies and food to missionaries in sixteen countries. She often received urgent calls to transport sick or injured people from remote mission stations to faraway hospitals.

Betty served as a missionary pilot for sixteen years. She was respected for her strong faith and passion for flying.

Ruby Bridges Hall
Courageous Desegregationist

{ 1954–PRESENT }

It took a lot of guts for six-year-old Ruby Bridges to begin first grade in 1960. She'd been selected to be one of the first African-American children to attend an all-white school in Louisiana. A lot of people were so angry about this that Ruby had to be driven to school and escorted inside by US marshals.

Her mother was pleased that Ruby had been chosen, but Ruby's father feared there would be trouble. And there was.

Each morning, Ruby was met by jeering crowds shouting obscenities and making threats. Ruby and her teacher, Mrs. Henry, were the only two in the classroom because the parents of the other first graders wouldn't allow their children to attend class with Ruby.

Ruby's mother told her to pray when she felt afraid, so Ruby did. She even prayed for the mean people shouting hateful words at her. Ruby never missed a day of school that year. The marshals were impressed by her courage, noting that Ruby never cried or whined.

The next year, other African-American students were admitted to the school, and there were no protesters. Ruby later graduated from an integrated high school and went to business school. She worked as a travel agent, married, and had children of her own.

Today she speaks in classrooms all over the country telling students, "Out of the commandments, the one you should keep is 'love thy neighbor.' That is the key."[5]

Ruby Bridges Hall

Hannah More

Writer and Philanthropist

{ 1745–1833 }

Hannah More was the fourth of five daughters born to Jacob and Mary More in England. The sisters were exceptionally bright—particularly Hannah, who loved to write from an early age. She often asked for paper for her birthday.

After writing her first school play when she was eighteen, Hannah began writing plays for the London stage. Witty and charming, she easily made friends with famous actors and other celebrities. Many of them did not share her Christian faith. Hannah sought to win them over with wit and reason. She wrote bestselling books, which were more popular than Jane Austen's novels at the time. Wealthy and popular, Hannah became one of the most influential women of her day.

Soon Hannah accepted a marriage proposal from a rich, older man. But when her fiancé postponed the wedding several times, Hannah became impatient and decided not to marry him. Instead, she devoted herself to charity projects, including supporting schools in poverty-stricken villages.

After meeting politician William Wilberforce, Hannah's life changed. She gave up her glamorous lifestyle to join Wilberforce and other Christian evangelicals in the Clapham Circle, dedicated to abolishing the slave trade. For many years, Hannah used her fame and social connections to win important supporters to the cause. She wrote persuasively to awaken her countrymen to the plight of the African slaves.

Hannah died at the age of eighty-seven, just a few weeks after her friend Wilberforce. Fortunately, both lived to see Parliament abolish slavery in the British Empire.

HANNAH MORE

Gabrielle "Gabby" Douglas
Olympic Gymnast

{ 1995–PRESENT }

When Gabby Douglas was a toddler, she flipped and tumbled everywhere. She even mastered the one-handed cartwheel, so her mother enrolled Gabby in gymnastics. She won the Virginia State Gymnastics Championship when she was eight years old. Everyone knew she was on her way to an Olympic gold medal.

At the age of fourteen, Gabby moved from Virginia to Iowa, where she lived with a host family so she could train with celebrated coach Liang Chow. Gabby worked hard. She attracted attention at national competitions, earning the nickname the Flying Squirrel because of the breathtaking heights she achieved while performing on the uneven bars.

But Gabby grew homesick. She wanted to quit. Everyone urged her to stick it out, reminding her the Olympics were just around the corner. With her family's encouragement and her Christian faith, Gabby found the power to persevere. She memorized Bible verses that inspired her while she practiced.

At age sixteen, Gabby earned worldwide fame at the 2012 Olympics Games in London when she became the first American to claim gold medals in the team and individual all-around events, as well as the first African American to win the individual all-around title.

Gabby competed again at the 2016 Olympic Games in Rio de Janeiro. She helped her team win a gold medal with her skilled performance on the uneven bars, inspiring the release of a Gabby Douglas Barbie doll that same year.

"All the glory goes to God," Gabby says.[6]

Amy Carmichael
Missionary to India

{ 1867–1951 }

Although she never married or had children, Amy Carmichael was *amma* ("mother") to hundreds of girls in India, where she served as a missionary for more than fifty years.

Amy was born into a wealthy family in Ireland. Her father owned numerous flour mills, but when he died, the family lost their wealth. Amy quit school to help raise her six younger siblings.

As an adult, Amy went to India to be a missionary. One day a little girl escaped from a Hindu temple and begged Amy to keep her safe. Amy knew the child lived a life of hardship and degradation, so she agreed to keep her.

The angry locals accused Amy of kidnapping. They demanded that she return the child, but Amy refused. From that day, she began to rescue other temple girls. She learned difficult Indian dialects and dressed in Indian clothing. She darkened her skin with coffee so she could travel to the temples without being recognized. Although she'd wanted blue eyes when she was a little girl, Amy now realized her brown eyes were perfect for India.

Throughout her ministry, Amy met with dangerous opposition. That did not prevent her from rescuing temple children. In 1931, she had a serious fall that left her an invalid. Amy continued to serve by writing books and devoting herself to prayer.

Known for her sweet disposition, Amy is remembered as one of the most beloved missionaries of all time. She reminded others, "You can give without loving, but you cannot love without giving."[7]

Sabina Wurmbrand

Voice of the Martyrs

{ 1913–2000 }

Torture. Starvation. Imprisonment. Sabina Wurmbrand survived them all.

Sabina was born into an Orthodox Jewish family in 1913 in Romania. When she was seventeen years old, her parents sent her to college in Paris. Happy to be away from her family's strict religious rules, Sabina wanted to have fun. She dated many men and eventually fell in love. She told Richard Wurmbrand she wanted to live only for pleasure. He agreed.

However, after they married, they converted to the Christian faith. The couple dedicated themselves to teaching other Jews about Jesus. When the Nazis invaded their city in World War II, Sabina and Richard were urged to flee. They didn't, and Sabina endured many hardships during the war. Her parents and siblings died in a concentration camp.

After the German army left, Russian soldiers invaded Romania. Sabina urged her husband to speak out against the Communists, who insisted there was no God. When Richard pointed out the risks, she said, "I do not need a coward for a husband."[8]

Richard and Sabina were imprisoned. Despite the hardships, Sabina's faith in Christ never faltered. She admitted, "Doing the work of God is dangerous. Not doing it is more dangerous."[9]

Finally, Christians from Norway secured the couple's freedom. In America, Richard testified before the US Senate about the inhumane treatment of prisoners behind the Iron Curtain.

Together, the Wurmbrands founded the Voice of the Martyrs. This organization helps Christians in countries where believers are persecuted for their faith.

Sabina Wurmbrand

Harriet Ross Tubman

American Abolitionist

{ 1820–1913 }

Born a slave on a Maryland plantation, Harriet Ross lived in a one-room cabin with her parents and eight brothers and sisters. Her mother worked as a cook in the plantation house and taught Harriet many Bible stories. Life was hard. Put to work at the age of six, Harriet was often lashed with a whip. When she was thirteen, she sustained a head injury that caused her to suffer from dizzy spells and headaches for the rest of her life.

In 1844, Harriet married John Tubman, a free black man. Longing to be free too, Harriet escaped to Pennsylvania in 1849. It was not easy. She couldn't read or write, and she didn't have a map. A woman of strong faith, Harriet gave credit to God for guiding her through danger. She said, "I always told God, I'm going to hold steady on you, and you've got to see me through."[10]

With the help of a secret network of men and women known as the Underground Railroad, Harriet returned to Maryland to rescue her family. She made many such trips and is credited with leading 300 slaves to freedom, earning the nickname "Moses." She was so successful that a reward of $40,000 was offered for her capture.

During the Civil War, Harriet served as a spy for the Union Army. The soldiers admired her courage and strong Christian faith. The US Treasury has considered releasing a newly designed $20 bill featuring Harriet's image.

HARRIET ROSS TUBMAN

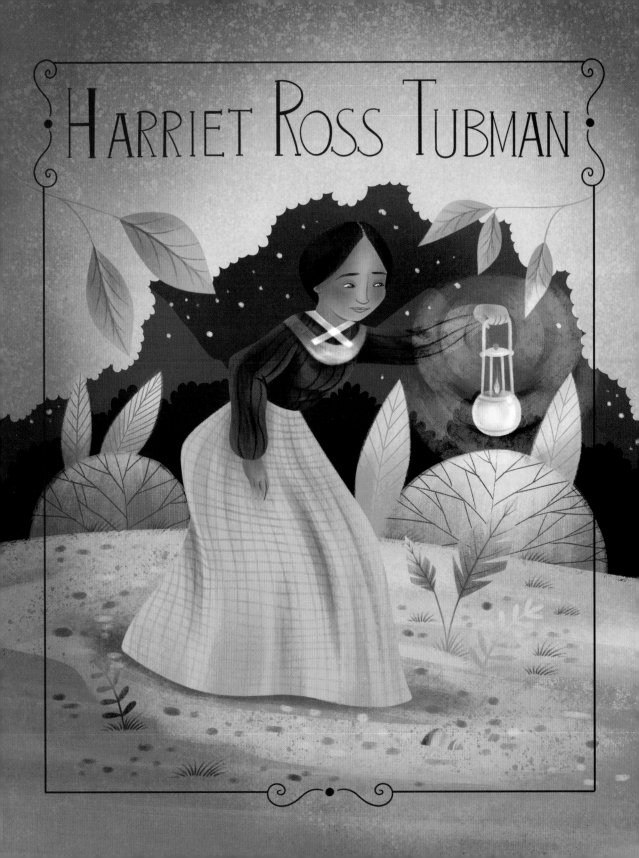

Lydia Darragh

Patriot Spy

{ 1729–1789 }

Lydia Darragh didn't look like a spy. She wore a plain gray Quaker dress and a white cap. She used old-fashioned words, like "thee" and "thou." Lydia was almost fifty years old in 1777 when General Howe's British troops moved in across the street from her Philadelphia home.

The British knew Quakers didn't fight in wars. But Howe's men didn't know that the Darraghs' oldest son, Charles, had disobeyed the Quaker position on nonviolence by enlisting in George Washington's colonial army.

Lydia often spied on the British across the street. She hid secret messages behind coat buttons on her fourteen-year-old son John and then sent him to deliver them.

One night, General Howe demanded to use the Darraghs' parlor for a staff meeting, and the family was ordered upstairs. Lydia eavesdropped. When she heard their plan to attack Washington's troops in nearby Whitemarsh, she devised a plan too.

The next morning, clutching an empty flour sack, Lydia left the city. When stopped by sentries, she explained she was on her way to the mill to buy flour.

Lydia trudged more than six miles that cold December day before she was able to relay her urgent news. When the British attacked, the Americans were ready. After three days of fighting, the British retreated. They didn't know that a plucky woman had foiled their plans.

Had the Americans not been alerted, Washington's war-weary troops might have been defeated, ending the colonists' fight for independence.

LYDIA DARRAGH

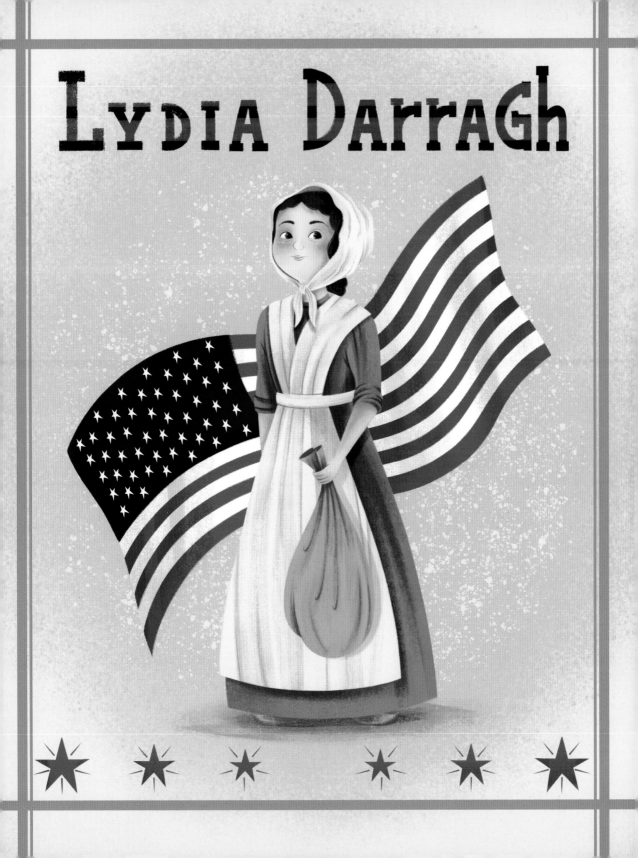

Ni Kwei-Tseng Soong
Mother of Christian China

{ 1869–1931 }

Ni Kwei-Tseng, nicknamed "Mamie," was born into a family of wealthy Christian Chinese scholars and government officials. She was lively but plain looking. Her parents assumed Mamie would never find a husband. Curious and intelligent, Mamie attended a missionary school, where she developed a love of math, learned to play the piano, and acquired a strong faith in Christ.

At the age of eighteen, Mamie's friends introduced her to a Chinese missionary named Charlie Soong, who had earned a theology degree from Vanderbilt University in the United States. Everyone was surprised but pleased when Charlie proposed. Mamie brought a large dowry to the marriage, and many American missionaries and important Chinese citizens from Shanghai attended the wedding.

Charlie started a successful business printing Chinese Bibles for the American Bible Society while Mamie raised the couple's six children—three girls and three boys. A strict disciplinarian, Mamie insisted that her daughters not have their feet bound in the traditional but crippling way. She also sent her sons and daughters to be educated at American universities when they were of age.

Mamie remained faithful all her life, spending hours in prayer each day in an upper room in the family's home. When her husband or children asked for her advice, she would reply, "I must ask God first."[11] The Soong children grew up to be prominent citizens in business and politics in modern China. Her daughter Mei-ling married General Chiang Kai-shek, who later became president of Taiwan.

Phillis Wheatley
Abolitionist Poet

{ 1753–1784 }

Phillis Wheatley was named after the slave ship that brought her to America at the age of seven. She was frail and sickly with skinny legs. She couldn't speak English. Moved by pity, a wealthy Boston couple, Susanna and John Wheatley, purchased the little girl.

The oldest Wheatley daughter taught Phillis the alphabet. Pleased by Phillis's quick intellect, the Wheatleys began teaching her astronomy, geography, history, English, and Latin. Phillis could read the Bible fluently by the time she was ten. She accepted Christ as her Savior while a teenager. When attending church services with the Wheatleys, Phillis had to sit in the pews reserved for slaves.

Phillis loved writing poems. In 1770, she wrote a poem about the death of a popular evangelist named George Whitefield. When it was published, Phillis became famous. In 1775, she wrote a poem praising General George Washington. When they met the following year, Phillis boldly encouraged him to consider freeing all slaves after the American Revolution.

With the help of a sympathetic countess in England, Phillis's collection of abolitionist poetry was published in Great Britain, making Phillis the first American slave to have a book published. Her fame spread.

When Mr. Wheatley died, Phillis became emancipated (set free). She helped organize missionary efforts for Ghana and Sierra Leone in Africa. Phillis then married a free black man named John Peters. Sadly, she died at the age of thirty-one after a difficult childbirth. Her stirring poetry is still read today.

Catherine Booth

Mother of the Salvation Army

{ 1829–1890 }

Catherine Mumford suffered from spine, lung, and heart trouble as a child in England, but illness did not prevent her from becoming one of the most influential women in religious history. Sweet-tempered and bright, Catherine read the Bible from cover to cover eight times before she turned twelve. She took an interest in social reform in her teens and served as secretary for the Juvenile Temperance Society, promoting abstinence from alcohol.

She met her husband, a preacher named William Booth, at a temperance meeting. The couple married in 1855 and had eight children. Together, they founded the Salvation Army, an organization dedicated to preaching the gospel and serving the poor.

Catherine was a bold and fiery orator. With William's support, she spoke at revivals and other church meetings. Her popularity soared, and she became more in demand as a speaker. The money she earned financed soup kitchens and homes for delinquent girls.

Soon Catherine began recruiting young women to serve as street preachers in slums and on the docks. The Hallelujah Lassies wore military-style uniforms. Their mission was to bring a saving knowledge of Christ to alcoholics, opium addicts, and wayward women.

Seven of the Booth children grew up to become high-ranking officials in the organization. Their daughter Evangeline Booth journeyed across the sea to organize a chapter of the Salvation Army in America. When Catherine died of cancer, nearly 40,000 mourners attended her funeral. The Salvation Army continues to serve the needy around the world today.

{ Catherine Booth }

Tamika Catchings Smith

Professional Basketball Star

{ 1979–PRESENT }

Born with a hearing disability, Tamika Catchings grew up with slurred speech and large, box-shaped hearing aids. At school, her classmates made fun of her. Tamika, shy and withdrawn, felt happiest at home shooting hoops with her older sister.

Tamika told her dad that when she grew up, she wanted to play for the National Basketball Association (NBA). When her father told her there were no women players, Tamika, undaunted, posted the words, "One day I will be in the NBA" on her bathroom mirror.

Her parents divorced when Tamika was in sixth grade, compounding her feelings of insecurity. Only on the basketball court did she feel strong and confident. In high school, she impressed everyone with her athletic abilities, winning numerous trophies and medals.

While playing basketball for the University of Tennessee, Tamika realized she wanted a closer relationship with Jesus. A knee injury provided her with time to focus on spiritual matters rather than sports.

Tamika was offered a contract to play for the Indiana Fever, a WNBA team, after graduating from college. She became an all-star, breaking multiple WNBA records and earning a spot on Team USA to compete in four Olympic Games, where she won four gold medals.

After retiring, Tamika married former basketball player Parnell Smith in 2016. She bought a teashop and enjoys being a sports analyst. Although proud of her accomplishments on the court, Tamika admits, "Being in church is what I want to do and what is important to me. It feeds my soul."[12]

Tamika Catchings Smith

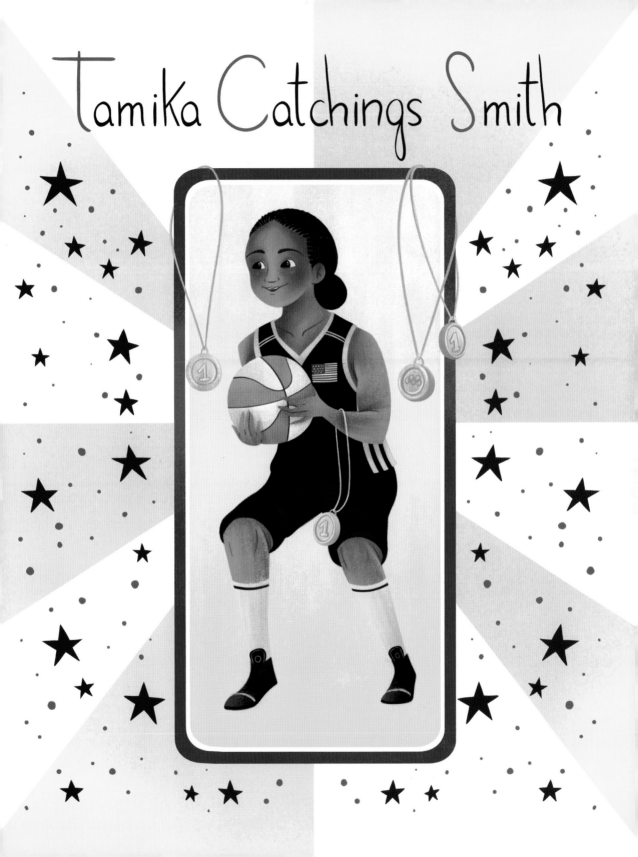

Mahalia Jackson
Gospel Music Queen

{ 1911–1972 }

Born into a large, devout Christian family in New Orleans, Mahalia Jackson began singing at church when she was four years old. By the time she was twelve, her soulful voice was so powerful, her singing could be heard all the way down the block.

Mahalia moved to Chicago in her teens. She joined a church choir and supplemented her income by singing at funerals and revivals. She soon gained a reputation for her heartfelt performances.

She recorded her first hit, "Moving On Up a Little Higher," in 1947. As her fame grew, Mahalia never forgot her faith, saying, "Faith and prayer are the vitamins of the soul; man cannot live in health without them."[13] When record producers urged her to sing jazz, she refused. She'd promised early in her life to sing only gospel music.

In 1950, she made history by singing at Carnegie Hall during the first Negro Music Gospel Festival. She performed the national anthem at the inauguration of President John F. Kennedy in 1961. With growing fame came financial success. But when Mahalia bought a home in a Chicago suburb, her neighbors threatened her. They didn't want an African American living there.

Having endured the indignities of segregation, Mahalia became a champion of civil rights. At his request, she joined Martin Luther King Jr. in his March on Washington in 1963, singing hymns before his speech.

Mahalia died in 1972. Thousands of mourners viewed her coffin. Aretha Franklin performed Mahalia's favorite hymn, "Precious Lord, Take My Hand."

Fanny Crosby

Hymn Writer

{ 1820–1915 }

Fanny Crosby was the most prolific female hymn writer of all time. Born in New York in 1820, she was blinded when she was just a baby after a doctor mistakenly applied the wrong medicine to her infected eyes. Despite her disability, Fanny was a happy and active little girl. She loved being outdoors. She loved poetry too. She was only eight years old when she wrote her first poem. She had an amazing memory and enjoyed reciting Bible verses. She memorized five chapters of the Bible each week from age ten, and by the time she was a teenager, Fanny had memorized the first five books of the Old Testament, all four Gospels, the book of Proverbs, and many psalms.

Fanny became a student at the New York Institution for the Blind when she was fifteen. After graduation, she was hired to be an English teacher there, but she still found time to write poems. She also wrote verses to put to music.

Over the years, Fanny wrote thousands and thousands of songs and hymns. They were sung at church services and crusades across the country. Many became so popular, they are still in hymnals today.

Fanny never resented her blindness. She once said, "When I get to heaven, the first face that shall ever gladden my sight will be that of my Savior."[14]

Catherine of Siena
Patron Saint of Europe

{ 1347–1380 }

B e who God meant you to be," Catherine of Siena advised, "and you will set the world on fire."[15]

That's exactly what she did.

Born Caterina Benincasa in the Tuscany region of Italy, Catherine grew up urging people to love God with all their hearts. A lively, joyful child with beautiful golden-brown hair, Catherine was just six years old when she received her first vision of Christ seated on the throne of glory.

From that moment she became quiet and solitary. She resisted her parents' efforts to dress her in fine gowns and jewels. When they arranged a marriage for her, Catherine cut her long hair and joined the Third Order of Saint Dominic, which allowed her to become a member of a religious order while living at home. The Dominican sisters taught her to read.

At twenty-one, Catherine received another vision. She became bolder, evangelizing among the poor and imprisoned. When the bubonic plague, or black death, swept through Siena, she earned respect by nursing the worst cases.

Popular and admired, Catherine wrote hundreds of sermons and letters urging repentance. She reminded others that Christ's love, not the nails, held Him to the cross. She became involved in politics, negotiating peace between warring city-states.

Catherine gained such a reputation for holiness, even the pope listened to her advice. At the age of thirty-three, Catherine died from a stroke, dictating words of spiritual encouragement to the very end.

In 1999, Catherine of Siena was named the patron saint of Europe.

Dorothy Day
Radical Reformer

{ 1897–1980 }

Dorothy Day was almost nine years old when an earthquake devastated San Francisco in 1906. She watched as community members pitched tents for the homeless and shared food. She never forgot how her neighbors helped one another.

Growing up, Dorothy cared little for God or religion. At the University of Illinois, she fell in with radical Communist students. Bored with classes, she dropped out and moved to New York, where she adopted an unconventional lifestyle and worked as a journalist. Dorothy was often jailed for participating in unlawful demonstrations. In 1917, she was arrested with other suffragists (people supporting women's right to vote) for protesting in front of the White House.

After accepting the existence of God through the beauty of his creation, Dorothy began reading the Bible and attending Mass. In 1927, she gave birth to a daughter, Tamar, whom she wanted to raise in the church.

Because of her new faith, Dorothy changed her lifestyle. In 1933, she cofounded the Catholic Worker Movement with Peter Maurin. She published the *Catholic Worker* newspaper, hoping to influence young people to improve society. Dorothy established hospitality houses for the homeless and advocated simple living. She promoted nonviolence, even after the bombing of Pearl Harbor during World War II.

When Dorothy visited Mother Teresa in India, they discussed ways to serve Christ. Dorothy said, "Do what comes to hand. Whatsoever thy hand finds to do, do it with all thy might. After all, God is with us."[16]

Today there are more than 200 Dorothy Day hospitality homes in the United States.

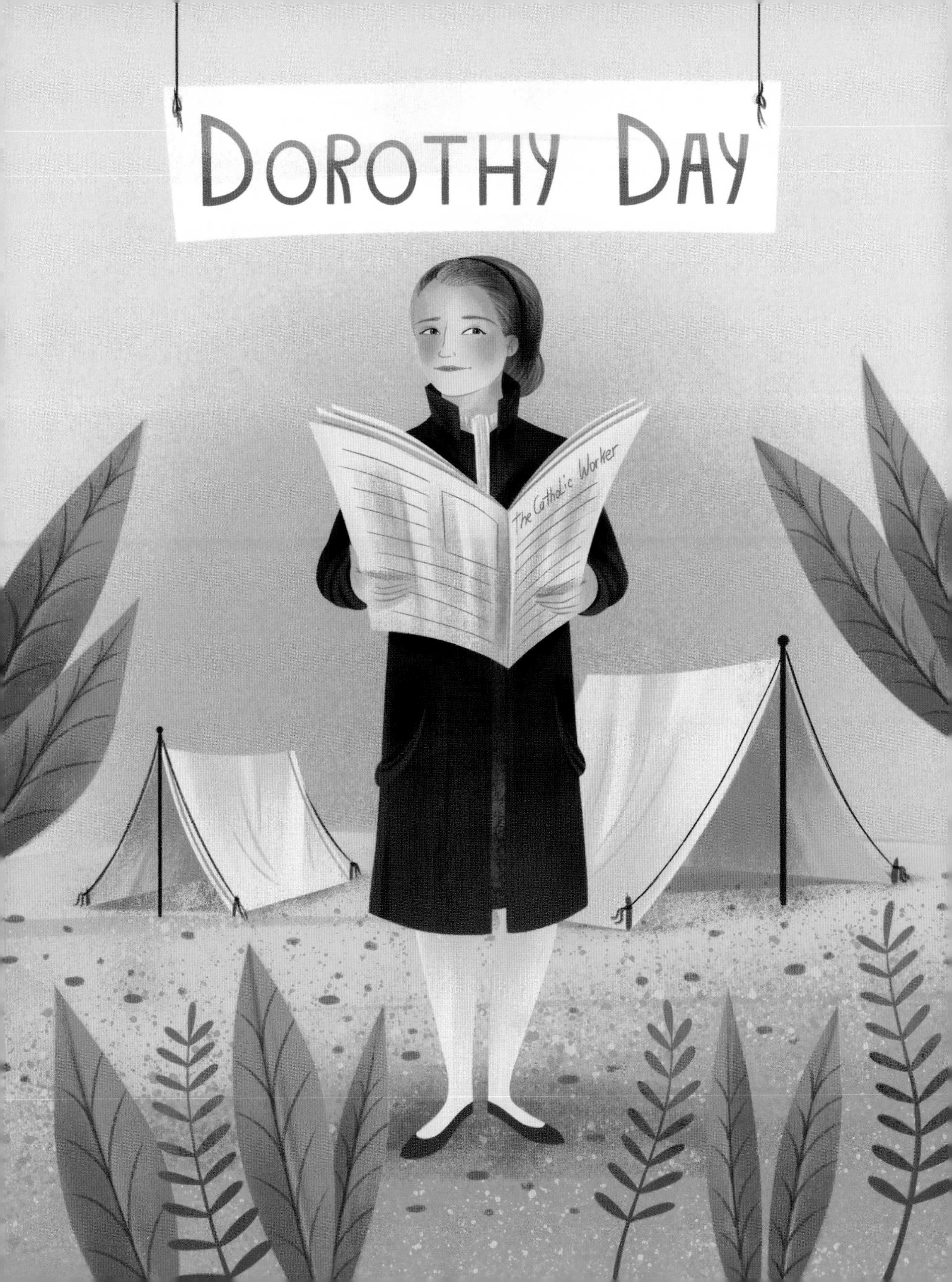
DOROTHY DAY
The Catholic Worker

Josephine Butler
Social Worker

{ 1826–1906 }

Josephine Butler fought to protect downtrodden women and girls. She grew up in a deeply religious and politically active British family. At age twenty-six, Josephine married George Butler, a scholar and Christian minister. With her husband's encouragement, she befriended unwed mothers and read the Bible in workhouses where women and children toiled like slaves.

When exposed to the horrors of human trafficking, Josephine started petition drives demanding laws to protect helpless victims. Josephine invited street women into her home until she could secure respectable jobs for them. After gaining financial support from public figures, including Florence Nightingale, Josephine established the House of Rest, where women could receive free health care and shelter.

She campaigned to help women go to school and find jobs. At the time, women were expected to be wives and mothers only. But Josephine pointed to the plight of two million single women in England, where there were not enough husbands to go around. She demanded to know how they were to honorably support themselves.

Josephine's ministry was a controversial one. Angry citizens flung rocks through her windows. They smeared her with dung. Her activities threatened her family's respectability and her husband's job. She bravely struggled on, saying, "I felt very weak and lonely, but there was One who stood by me."[17]

Her dedication paid off. Josephine was appointed president of the North England Council for Higher Education for Women in 1867 and lived to see the establishment of the first women's college at Cambridge.

Rosa Parks
Civil Rights Heroine

{ 1913–2005 }

Racism was ever present when Rosa Macauley grew up in Alabama. White children called her names and threw rocks at her as she walked to the cotton fields in bare feet. Rosa recited Psalm 27 when she needed courage.

She loved attending classes at the Montgomery Industrial School for Girls. Rosa dreamed of being a teacher but dropped out to care for her sick grandmother.

At age eighteen, she met Raymond Parks, a barber. After they married, he encouraged her to earn her high school diploma. Together, they took an interest in civil rights activities.

One December day in 1955, Rosa boarded a bus after work. When the driver ordered her to give up her seat for a white man, she politely said no. She'd put up with discrimination all her life. She said, "As a child, I learned from the Bible to trust in God and not be afraid."[18] On that fateful day, she trusted God to get her through the ordeal.

Rosa was arrested, but her simple act of courage set in motion events that changed history. Thousands of citizens launched a bus boycott that lasted 385 days. Laws changed. A year later, Rosa legally sat in a front seat on a bus. The 1964 Civil Rights Act outlawed segregation of public accommodations, such as restrooms and elevators.

Rosa received many awards during her lifetime. She encouraged others, saying, "You must never be fearful about what you're doing when it is right."[19]

Rosa Parks

Anne Bradstreet
Pilgrim Poet

{ 1612–1672 }

Anne Bradstreet had a passion for poetry. She wrote about God, nature, and her affection for her beloved husband, Simon, whom she married when she was sixteen.

She grew up on an earl's comfortable estate in England, where her father worked as the manager. At a young age, Anne learned to read the Bible as well as Greek and British classics. She once wrote, "When I was about seven…I had at one time eight tutors…in languages, music, dancing."[20]

In 1630, the young newlyweds and Anne's parents immigrated to the New World with other Puritans to join a settlement in Salem, Massachusetts. Anne was disheartened by the primitive living conditions and the scarcity of food. She was often sick. Anne poured out her thoughts and feelings in her poems. Some people criticized her for writing when there was so much work to do, but that didn't stop her.

Despite poor health, Anne gave birth to eight children. Her husband became the governor of the Massachusetts Bay Colony. Even though Anne had many responsibilities, she always found time to write. Sometimes she wrote love poems for Simon. She also wrote about sin and salvation and cleaning house.

When Anne's brother-in-law had her collection of poems printed in London in 1650, Anne became the first New England colonist to have a book published. Many people in England and America read *The Tenth Muse Lately Sprung Up in America*. Even King George was said to own a copy at his palace.

ANNE BRADSTREET

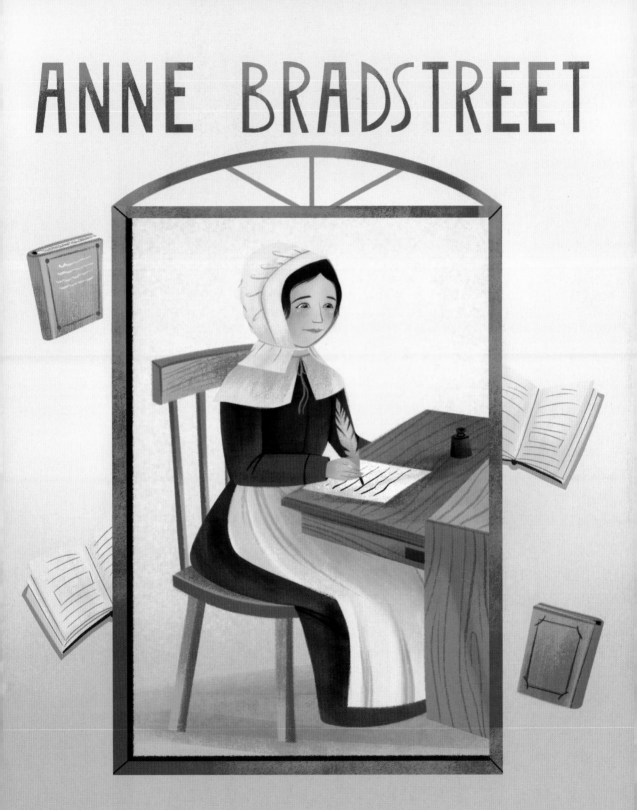

Bethany Hamilton
Spirited Surfer

{ 1990–PRESENT }

Bethany Hamilton was born to surf. She grew up in Hawaii, where her parents and two older brothers participated in the sport. No one was surprised when the little girl took to the surfboard like a champ, winning her first competition when she was just eight.

Homeschooled by her mother so she could spend more time competing, Bethany was thirteen years old when a tiger shark bit off her left arm. She lost nearly half her blood, but friends rushed her to the hospital, where she endured multiple surgeries.

Relying on her Christian faith and courage, Bethany returned to the water with her surfboard in less than a month following the attack. One year later, she amazed the sporting world by winning the Explorer Women's division of the 2005 NSSA National Championships.

Bethany's first book, *Soul Surfer*, became a national bestseller, inspiring a major motion picture. The loss of her arm has been no obstacle. She has become one of the world's greatest professional surfers. "Being out there in the ocean, God's creation, it's like a gift He has given us to enjoy," she wrote.[21]

In 2013, Bethany married youth pastor Adam Dirks. The couple has a baby boy. She continues to inspire others through writing and public appearances. Her foundation, Friends of Bethany, supports other shark-attack victims and amputees. She is an active member of Christian Surfers International, which is committed to sharing the gospel with the surfing community.

Christine Caine

Halting Human Trafficking

{ 1966–PRESENT }

G rowing up in Australia, Christine Caryofyllis had a troubled childhood. Bullied at school and abused by adults, she lived in fear. After reading the Bible, she clung to her unshakable faith in Jesus to see her through difficult times. Christine earned a degree in English from the University of Sydney and met her husband, Nick Caine, during Bible study at church. The evangelist was in her thirties when she discovered she'd been adopted after being abandoned as an infant by her birth parents.

Her heart-wrenching experiences caused her to be sympathetic to the plight of helpless victims of human trafficking. When Christine learned that two million children are sold each year around the globe, she made up her mind to combat the crime. Christine and her husband formed the A21 Campaign in 2008. This organization is dedicated to raising awareness about the issue, providing rehabilitation and care for survivors and taking legal action against traffickers.

Inspired by Jesus's instruction in Matthew 9 to pray to the Lord of the harvest to send forth laborers, Christine later launched the Propel Women program in 2015 to encourage women to seek their potential to serve in God's kingdom.

Now one of the most well-known evangelists in the world, Christine has written several books and preaches at megachurches around the globe. She admonishes the "selfie" generation, "We have to fall in love with being a laborer. There is no higher honor than being a co-laborer with Jesus."[22]

Amanda Smith

The Orphans' Champion

{ 1837–1915 }

Born a slave in Maryland, Amanda Berry Smith was one of thirteen children. Her parents were married but lived on different plantations. They were devout believers and raised their children to love Jesus. At thirteen, Amanda performed the tasks of a housemaid. She was fifteen when her father purchased her freedom. Together they moved north to Pennsylvania.

Amanda married at seventeen. She endured poverty and hardship. Her husband enlisted in the Union Army during the Civil War but never returned. Four of her five children died as babies. Her second husband died from cancer. With each tragedy, Amanda drew closer to God.

When Amanda began her preaching ministry, she joyfully distributed Bible tracts on street corners. She sang at revivals. For forty years, both black and white Christians invited her to preach at their events.

Amanda became instrumental in the Women's Christian Temperance Union and helped to establish the National Association for the Advancement of Colored People (NAACP). Despite her popularity, Amanda felt the sting of racism, saying, "I think some people would understand the quintessence of sanctifying grace if they could be black about twenty-four hours."[23]

As her reputation grew, Amanda evangelized in Great Britain and India. She served as a missionary in Liberia in Africa for eight years. After returning to the United States, she raised funds to build an orphanage for destitute black children in 1899 in a small town near Chicago—the first establishment of its kind. She worked tirelessly for the rest of her life to support the orphanage.

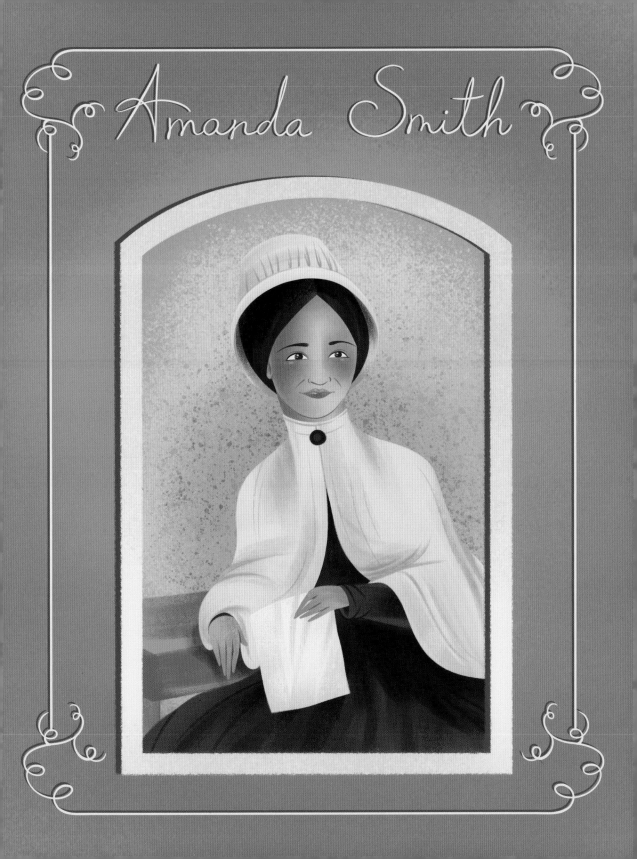

Amanda Smith

Jane Austen
Anonymous Novelist

{ 1775–1817 }

Preacher's kid. Spinster. British novelist.

Jane Austen grew up with seven brothers and sisters. Her father had a large library, which he encouraged the children to use. When Jane began writing plays at an early age, he gave her paper and quills to write with.

At age ten, Jane attended boarding school, where she studied music, dance, and foreign languages. When she finished, Jane returned home and never married. She attended church services with her parents, played the piano, and visited the poor. She was kind, humble, and witty.

Jane also attended dances and parties, frequently writing about these in her novels. Like most female authors at the time, Jane wrote anonymously. *Sense and Sensibility*, her first novel, was published in 1811. She used her writing income to support her mother and sister Cassandra after Reverend Austen died.

Her most popular novel, *Pride and Prejudice*, was published in 1813. Jane referred to it as her "darling child." Her books represented real life more so than most previous novels and set a precedent for future novelists to follow. Sometimes she wrote down her prayers: "Thou art everywhere present, from thee no secret can be hid. May the knowledge of this, teach us to fix our thoughts on thee with reverence and devotion that we pray not in vain."[24]

Not until after her death did her brother Henry reveal to the public that Jane had written the novels, which are still popular today.

Jeanette Li

Chinese Evangelist

{ 1899–1968 }

Jeanette Li was a disappointment to her father from the moment she was born. He'd wanted a son. But as Jeanette was his only child, her father raised her as he would a boy, sending her to a private school at the age of five—a rare opportunity for a Chinese female at the time.

While being treated for a serious illness at a mission hospital, Jeanette learned about Jesus and converted to Christianity. Her father had recently died, but her mother also accepted Christ and allowed Jeanette to continue her education at the mission school.

Relatives ostracized Jeanette and her mother following their conversion. Hoping to provide for her daughter's security, Jeanette's mother arranged a marriage for her at the age of sixteen. The marriage was not a happy one. When Jeanette's husband left her, she raised their son, Timothy, alone.

While registering for college, Jeanette was told she'd have to denounce her Christian faith. Tearing up the registration papers, she took a job with an American missionary organization to teach the gospel in remote Chinese villages.

After the Japanese invaded China, Jeanette suffered beatings and deprivations. Later, she endured imprisonment and starvation under the Communists. Still Jeanette clung to her faith.

She was eventually released from prison and came to the United States in 1962, where she ministered to a Chinese community in Los Angeles until her death. Despite many hardships, Jeanette proclaimed, "In every period of my life I have found God sufficient for my every need."[25]

Harriet Beecher Stowe

Literary Superstar

{ 1811–1896 }

When *Uncle Tom's Cabin* was published in 1852, one reviewer declared it "a verbal earthquake, an ink-and-paper tidal wave."[26] The characters Tom, Eva, and Topsy became iconic, and their creator, world famous.

Born a preacher's kid in Connecticut, Harriet Beecher was one of thirteen children raised in a religious family active in social causes and educational pursuits. No one was surprised when she gave her life to Christ at the age of fourteen.

In 1836, Harriet married Calvin Stowe, a Bible professor at Lane Seminary in Cincinnati, Ohio. Although busy raising their seven children, Harriet found time to write short stories to supplement the family's meager income.

At the time, the Stowes lived across the river from a slave-holding community in Kentucky. Friends told Harriet about a secret network of abolitionists who helped runaway slaves. Harriet brooded about what she could do to help the Underground Railroad. She felt outraged that so few ministers spoke out against the evils of slavery.

When friends encouraged her to write about it, Harriet mused, "The power of fictitious writing, for good as well as for evil, is a thing which ought most seriously to be reflected upon."[27]

One Sunday morning in church, Harriet had an idea. She quickly wrote the heart-wrenching novel *Uncle Tom's Cabin*. The book made insightful claims about the value of human souls. It sold more than one million copies before the Civil War.

Harriet's pen proved to be a powerful weapon in the fight for emancipation of America's slaves.

Florence Nightingale
Pioneer of Modern Nursing

{ 1820–1910 }

Florence Nightingale was a teenager when she saved the life of a shepherd's dog by tending to the animal's badly injured leg. Afterward, Florence believed she had a vision: "On February 7, 1837, God spoke to me and called me into his service."[28]

Born into a wealthy English family, Florence gave up society parties and European vacations to serve the sick. Her parents were horrified when Florence decided to pursue nursing. At the time, nursing was considered scandalous. Charity hospitals were unclean, and the women working there were said to be slovenly drunkards.

Undaunted, she read medical books and visited hospitals. Florence, beautiful and stylish, received many marriage proposals but refused them all. A friend told her, "You could have been a duchess." Florence shrugged, more interested in serving God by saving lives.

When the Crimean War broke out in 1853, Florence took three dozen trained nurses to the battlefield in Turkey. Under their care, the British soldiers' death rate dropped from 42 percent to 3 percent. Patients watching Florence tiptoe through the wards at midnight dubbed her "The Lady with the Lamp."

After the war, she visited Queen Victoria to share her experiences. With the queen's approval, Florence established the first military hospital and medical college. When illness caused her to become an invalid, Florence wrote nursing textbooks from her bed.

For her tireless efforts, Florence was awarded the Order of Merit, Britain's equivalent of America's Presidential Medal of Freedom. She was the first woman to receive this award.

Jennifer Wiseman

God's Stargirl

{ 1965–PRESENT }

Jennifer Wiseman grew up on an Arkansas farm. She loved animals and star-gazing. Her Christian parents raised her to appreciate God's beauty in creation. Each evening when the family took a walk around the farm, Jennifer admired the stars. At school, she was intrigued by photographs of the moons of Jupiter and Saturn taken during the Voyager mission probe.

After high school, Jennifer attended the Massachusetts Institute of Technology to study physics. In 1987, while working on a summer research project at the Lowell Observatory in Arizona, the budding astronomer discovered a new comet. It is appropriately named Comet 114P/Wiseman-Skiff. More fascinated than ever with stars, Jennifer pursued her doctoral degree in astronomy at Harvard.

Today, Dr. Wiseman is a senior astrophysicist at the NASA Goddard Space Flight Center. Her job is to supervise the Hubble Space Telescope mission. She works with hundreds of other scientists studying regions of the galaxy where stars formed, using radio, optical, and infrared telescopes. She shares Hubble's amazing discoveries in media throughout the world.

A devout Christian, Dr. Wiseman has written essays addressing the relationship between Christian faith and astronomy. She says, "It's glorious actually, when you think about the fact that the atoms in our bodies were literally forged in stars. As a person of faith myself, I think of stars as God's factories."[29]

Jennifer is married to Dr. Mark Shelhamer, also a scientist with NASA. She enjoys giving talks about astronomy and God's creation in schools, church youth groups, and civic organizations.

Pocahontas

Dove of Peace

{ 1595–1617 }

Most elementary students learn the story of Pocahontas, who saved the life of English colonist John Smith by throwing herself over him to prevent his execution. The remainder of her life proves just how plucky she was.

The favorite daughter of Chief Powhatan, who ruled numerous tribes in the Tidewater region of Virginia, Pocahontas had an ordinary childhood. She played games, foraged for food, gathered firewood, and helped with cooking.

When the English colonists established Jamestown in 1607, everything changed. Frequent skirmishes broke out between the tribes and the colonists. When Powhatan's warriors captured English soldiers, the colonists took Pocahontas hostage. They offered to exchange her for the English prisoners.

These negotiations took many months. Meanwhile, pastor Alexander Whitaker used the Bible to teach Pocahontas how to read and speak English. Embracing the Christian faith, she was baptized in 1614, taking the name Rebecca. She also married a widower named John Rolfe.

Now a farmer's wife, Rebecca Rolfe soon gave birth to a baby, Thomas. The marriage helped establish peace between the settlers and native tribes.

In 1616, the Rolfes traveled to England for a visit. The arrival of the vivacious "Indian Princess" caused quite a stir. Even King James I wanted to meet Rebecca Rolfe, the toast of London society. A year later, as the Rolfe family prepared to return to Jamestown, Rebecca became ill and died.

Today a huge painting by artist John Gadsby Chapman, depicting her baptism, hangs on the wall in the Capitol building in Washington, DC.

Pocahontas

Joni Eareckson Tada

Champion for the Disabled

{ 1949–PRESENT }

In high school, Joni Eareckson enjoyed athletics, especially swimming and horseback riding. But in 1967, she broke her neck in a tragic diving accident that left her paralyzed from the neck down and confined to a wheelchair.

For many years, Joni struggled with despair, wondering what God wanted her to do. She eventually found peace and spiritual strength through intense Bible study. Joni was also inspired by the life of Helen Keller, who did not let deafness and blindness prevent her from achieving her life's goals.

Joni taught herself to paint, holding the brush in her mouth, and soon earned a reputation as a talented mouth artist. She is also a gifted vocalist, radio host, and author. Joni met Ken Tada at church, and the couple married in 1982. To encourage others with disabilities, Joni established the Joni and Friends International Disability Center in California, an organization that advances Christian ministries to the disabled around the world.

As an advocate for the disabled, Joni accepted a presidential appointment to the National Council on Disability and served for several years. Joni has also received many honors and awards. For her efforts to promote evangelism among the disabled, the National Association of Evangelicals named her Layperson of the Year in 1986—the first woman to receive the honor.

Although still confined to a wheelchair, Joni continues to walk with Christ, saying, "I have found limitless joy and peace in knowing the Lord Jesus."[30]

JONI EARECKSON TADA

Madeleine L'Engle
Bold Storyteller

{ 1918–2007 }

Madeleine L'Engle began writing stories as soon as she could hold a pencil.

Born in New York, Madeleine felt unpopular at school. One teacher called her stupid. When she won a poetry contest in fifth grade, the teacher accused Madeleine of plagiarism. At age twelve, she moved with her parents to Europe, where she attend a boarding school in Switzerland. In 1941, she graduated from college with an English degree and moved to New York to work in the theater, writing stories and plays and acting. She married actor Hugh Franklin, and the couple had three children.

Madeleine wrote children's books too, including *A Wrinkle in Time*, an idea that came to her on a family camping trip. Twenty-six publishers rejected the controversial novel before it was published. After it won the prestigious Newbery Medal in 1963, the book sold more than 14 million copies and inspired four sequels.

Madeleine considered herself a devout Christian, spending time daily reading the Bible and praying, but some critics declared her books anti-Christian. On the other hand, others criticized her novels for being too religious. Both attitudes annoyed Madeline. "Jesus was not a theologian. He was God who told stories," she said.[31] Madeleine often felt surprised when some schools and libraries banned her books.

Despite her busy writing schedule, Madeleine found time to serve as the librarian for the Cathedral Church of Saint John the Divine for more than thirty years. She died peacefully in a nursing home at the age of 89.

Madeleine L'Engle

Narcissa Whitman
Oregon Trail Missionary

{ 1808–1847 }

Narcissa Prentiss was one of nine children born to Stephen and Clarissa Prentiss in rural New York. Bright and well educated, Narcissa made up her mind at age sixteen to evangelize Native Americans in the West. At the time, unmarried women were not encouraged to be missionaries. When Marcus Whitman learned of her desire to serve, he proposed. They married in 1836 and began their wagon train trek the next day.

The 2000-mile journey proved long and difficult. Narcissa was enchanted by God's creation, but she lamented the loss of many of her belongings along the way. She gave birth to their only child, Alice, when the travelers reached Oregon Territory.

The missionaries began serving immediately. "Our desire is to be useful to these benighted Indians, teaching them the way of salvation," Narcissa wrote.[32] She had a beautiful soprano voice and sang during worship services. While Marcus served as minister and doctor, Narcissa ran the household and taught school. They also took in orphans.

Narcissa was heartbroken when baby Alice drowned in a stream. After eight long years, the missionaries grew frustrated by the lack of spiritual growth among the Cayuse. They offered to provide medical care when a plague devastated the tribe, but the Cayuse feared being poisoned. In November 1847, warriors attacked the mission, killing Marcus, Narcissa, and several others before taking most of the women and children as captives.

Years later, orphans cared for by the Whitmans recalled Narcissa's courage, her determination, and her love of picnics.

Narcissa Whitman

Nancy Pearcey
Preeminent Professor

{ 1952–PRESENT }

Nancy Randolph was raised in a religious home, but she doubted that Christianity was true and rejected her secondhand faith while in high school. Still, she was concerned that if God did not exist, life had no meaning. As a young adult, Nancy traveled to Europe to study the violin. While there, she visited the L'Abri Institute in Switzerland to study under the brilliant Christian scholar Francis A. Schaeffer.

This intellectual experience changed Nancy's life. She embraced a faith in Christ, boldly proclaiming God's truth. She earned multiple degrees, including a master's degree from Covenant Theological Seminary, and served as the Francis A. Schaeffer Scholar at the World Journalism Institute. For many years, she coauthored a worldview column with Chuck Colson for *Christianity Today* magazine.

Nancy met Richard Pearcey in Switzerland. They married in the United States several years later and have two sons, whom she homeschooled. Her bestselling books include *Total Truth*, *Finding Truth*, *The Soul of Science*, and *Saving Leonardo*. She has been a guest speaker at various universities, including Princeton, Stanford, and Dartmouth. She has lectured politicians at the US Capitol and the White House and addressed scientists at Los Alamos National Laboratory.

With a heart for young people seeking answers to their questions about faith, Nancy is pleased when Christian converts like hip-hop artist Lecrae, winner of multiple Dove and Grammy awards, quotes from her book *Total Truth* and corresponds with her through Facebook.

Today, Nancy is a professor at Houston Baptist University, teaching students to love the Lord with all their hearts, souls, and minds.

NANCY PEARCEY

Ida Lewis

America's Bravest Woman

{ 1842–1911 }

Ida Lewis grew up in a Rhode Island lighthouse. A strong swimmer and skilled at rowing small boats, she was only a teenager the first time she rescued someone who was drowning.

When she was fifteen, her father, Hosea Lewis, became wheelchair bound. That's when Ida began performing the duties at the Lime Rock Lighthouse (now the Ida Lewis Lighthouse). Twice a day, she climbed the tall staircase, filled the lamps with oil, trimmed the wick, and polished the reflectors.

One stormy night in March 1869, Ida's mother noticed a boat capsizing in the churning waves. She sent Ida and her younger brother out to help the struggling men.

One of them, seeing Ida, cried out in despair, "It's only a girl!"

But he was wrong—Ida wasn't *only* a girl. She'd already saved more than a dozen men from the stormy Rhode Island waters. She saved this man's life too, clutching his wet jacket and hauling him into her rowboat.

Because of her many daring rescues, Ida was dubbed "America's Bravest Woman." For her unstinting duty to the United States Lighthouse Service, she received many awards and honors. President Ulysses Grant traveled to Rhode Island to thank her for her service.

Ida was sixty-three years old when she dove into the harbor to make her last daring rescue. She died of a stroke six years later.

Shy and modest, Ida never enjoyed publicity. When someone asked her how she found the courage, Ida replied, "I don't know. I ain't particularly strong. The Lord Almighty gives me the strength when I need it, that's all."[33]

Condoleezza Rice
Influential Political Advisor

{ 1954–PRESENT }

Condoleezza Rice has often been first. She was a first and only child. She was the first musical prodigy in her Alabama community, giving an astounding piano recital at the age of four. She was the first student at her school to skip both first and seventh grades.

Because her father was a pastor and her mother the church organist, Condi spent a lot of time in church. Her Christian faith has always been a part of who she is. Her mother raised her to have confidence and to ignore racial slurs.

In college, Condi pursued a degree in political science. After earning a PhD, she taught classes at Stanford University. She was the first woman to be offered a fellowship to Stanford University's Center for International Security and Arms Control. As she gained a reputation as a foreign-policy expert, Condi became the first black woman to serve as a US security adviser for an American president, offering valuable advice to President George W. Bush following the 9/11 terrorist attacks.

She also became the first black woman to be appointed Secretary of State. During the Bush administration, she traveled half a million miles around the world, charming the press corps and strengthening relationships with America's allies.

When asked how her faith influenced her tough decisions, Condoleezza answered that "faith and reason are not enemies of one another, that indeed we are called to love the Lord our God with our hearts and our minds, by Scripture."[34]

Betty Olsen
Missionary Martyr

{ 1934–1969 }

As the daughter of American missionaries serving in Africa, Betty Olsen's childhood was often lonely and unhappy. Her mother died when she was a teenager, and Betty resented her father's second marriage. After studying nursing in the United States, she returned to Africa. Betty was so difficult to get along with, the missionaries asked her to leave.

At age 29, Betty felt bitter and suicidal. A Chicago youth minister helped her deal with her feelings by studying the Bible. Refreshed, she eagerly joined a mission team in Vietnam, ministering to lepers.

Friends and family expressed concern about Betty serving in Vietnam, where American troops were engaged in a war with Communist Vietcong troops. "I am very much at peace," Betty assured them. "I know that I may never come back, but I know that I am in the center of the Lord's will, and Vietnam is the place for me."[35]

In 1969, the Vietcong attacked the missionary compound, killing several members of the missionary team. Betty and the other captives endured humiliation and torture. They marched long hours through the steamy, insect-infested jungle and survived on meager rice rations. They suffered from fevers and bloodsucking leeches.

Betty used her nursing skills to help her friends, but after eight months of deprivation and illness, she died. The one missionary who survived the ordeal returned to the United States and shared how Betty Olsen had saved his life, demonstrating Christ's love even to those who abused her.

Betty Olsen

Mother Teresa

Nobel Prize–Winning Missionary

{ 1910–1997 }

Anjezë Gonxhe Bojaxhiu was born in present-day Skopje in the Republic of Macedonia. The youngest of three children, Agnes (the English form of her first name) enjoyed a happy childhood. The family attended church services daily. Fun loving and popular, Agnes enjoyed youth group activities.

When Agnes's father died unexpectedly, her mother worked as a seamstress to support her children. Always mindful of those less fortunate, the family often invited the homeless to dine with them. Agnes felt the Lord calling her to religious service. When she turned eighteen, she joined the Sisters of Loreto in Ireland, taking the name Mary Teresa. She was sent to India to teach at a girls' school. She frequently rescued dying people from gutters, but hospital personnel often refused to admit them.

Mother Teresa demanded a building where she could care for the dying in dignified comfort. But soon after the hospice was built, an angry crowd threatened to tear it down. Fearlessly, Mother Teresa invited the mob's leader inside to see how the nuns served others. Afterward, the shamefaced man dismissed the hostile crowd.

After establishing the Order of the Missionaries of Charity, Mother Teresa broadened her ministry to include abandoned babies and lepers. Donations poured in. Few refused when she asked, "Would you like to do something beautiful for God?"[36]

For her "outrageous courage," Mother Teresa received many awards, including the prestigious Nobel Peace Prize in 1979. Celebrities, including Diana, Princess of Wales, sought her advice. When Mother Teresa died in September 1997, India held a state funeral attended by dignitaries from around the world.

Clara Barton
Angel of the Battlefield

{ 1821–1912 }

Clara Barton was a shy little girl who spoke with a lisp. She dreamed of becoming a nurse. When her brother David fell from a barn roof, his doctors declared he'd never recover. Eleven-year-old Clara nursed him back to health.

Clara worked as a teacher for many years but became a nurse in 1861 after one of the first major battles of the Civil War. She started an organization that delivered supplies to the soldiers. Clara tended the wounded during the battles, earning the nickname "Angel of the Battlefield." On one occasion, a bullet whizzed through the sleeve of her dress, killing the soldier she was nursing.

Clara cared deeply for her patients. She wrote a letter to her cousin, saying, "[I wish] that Christ would teach my soul a prayer that would plead to the Father for grace sufficient" to comfort the dying men and their families.[37]

President Lincoln asked Clara to trace missing soldiers, and she spent four years doing so. She and her sister Sally answered 63,000 letters from families requesting help. After completing this monumental task, she traveled to Europe to recover her failing health.

While in Switzerland, Clara learned about the International Red Cross. The organization assisted homeless refugees during the Franco-Prussian War of 1871. Clara volunteered to help. When she returned to the United States, she established the American Red Cross and served as president for twenty-three years. Clara's legacy lives on today as the organization continues to serve veterans and help victims of floods, tornadoes, and other natural disasters.

Susan B. Anthony
Suffragist and Social Crusader

{ 1820–1906 }

Susan Brownell Anthony was a bright child. She learned to read and write at the age of three. Her father, the owner of a cotton mill, home-schooled Susan and her siblings. They were raised in a religious family in the Quaker tradition. Susan grew up believing everyone was created equal in the eyes of God—including women and black slaves.

When Susan turned eighteen, her father declared bankruptcy. Susan worked as a teacher to help support the family, earning three dollars a week. When she learned that male teachers earned three times as much as she did, she felt outraged. She became active in the temperance and antislavery movements. She spoke out for women's right to vote and own property. She gave lively speeches, passed out pamphlets, and testified before congressional committees.

In 1869, Susan and Elizabeth Cady Stanton established the National Woman Suffrage Association, which later merged with the National American Woman Suffrage Association. Susan endured name-calling from hostile mobs as well as many miles of uncomfortable travel as she campaigned for equal rights for women. When she voted illegally in the 1872 presidential election, she was arrested and fined.

In 1905, Susan met with President Theodore Roosevelt at the White House, seeking his endorsement for a constitutional amendment allowing women to vote. The Nineteenth Amendment passed in 1920, several years after Susan's death. In 1979, the US Treasury released a silver dollar coin depicting Susan's image.

Susan B. Anthony

Katherine G. Johnson

Space-Age Mathematician

{ 1918–2020 }

As a small child, Katherine Coleman loved to count and solve equations. She counted the number of steps from her house to her church. She counted forks and knives when she set the table. A math prodigy, she graduated from high school at the age of fourteen. Katherine was still a teenager when she graduated from college with degrees in math and French. She then became the first African American in the graduate program at West Virginia University.

Katherine's first husband, James Goble, died of a brain tumor in 1956. She married James Johnson in 1959.

In 1953, Katherine joined an all-black team of "human computers" for NASA's Project Mercury spaceflight program. Her math skills earned her a place on the main research team, where she produced calculations for the 1961 flight trajectory of astronaut Alan Shepard, the first American in space. She also verified the computer calculations for John Glenn's 1962 orbit and for the 1969 Apollo 11 trajectory to the moon.

Katherine's Christian faith provided a solid foundation on which she could build her extraordinary life. She exhibited patience, kindness, and civility to those who treated her with discrimination because she was black and female. She never felt inferior, confidently saying, "Girls are capable of doing everything men are capable of doing. Sometimes they have more imagination than men."[38]

In 2015, President Barack Obama awarded Katherine the Medal of Freedom, the nation's highest civilian award. The next year, the book *Hidden Figures* was published, revealing Katherine's (and other women's) contribution to the space program. The book led to an Oscar-nominated major motion picture.

Elizabeth Blackwell

Pioneering Physician

{ 1821–1910 }

Like her religious parents, Elizabeth Blackwell believed in helping others. She worked as a teacher, but when a sick friend admitted she was not comfortable being treated by an unsympathetic male physician, Elizabeth decided to become a doctor.

However, no medical school would accept her. When the Geneva Medical College in New York received Elizabeth's application, administrators thought it was a joke. They admitted her as a student, never expecting her to attend.

Elizabeth faced hostility every day. When told it was inappropriate for a woman to view a male corpse during a dissection, Elizabeth replied, "The human body is holy" and reminded the professor she had a right to attend his lecture.[39]

After graduating at the top of her class, Elizabeth became the first woman in the United States to receive a medical degree. When landlords refused to rent her office space, Elizabeth opened a clinic in her home to treat women and children.

Wanting more experience, Elizabeth went to France to work in a maternity hospital. There she developed an eye infection, resulting in the loss of vision in one eye. Returning to New York, she and her sister Emily, also a doctor, opened an infirmary in the slums. They believed many diseases could be prevented by proper hygiene and sanitation.

Elizabeth trained military nurses during the Civil War. After the war, she opened a hospital called the New York Infirmary for Indigent Women and Children. Elizabeth's persistence made it possible for other women to become doctors. Today 50 percent of medical students are women.

Joan of Arc
Military Hero

{ 1412–1431 }

The daughter of French peasants, Joan never went to school or learned to read. She fed the farm animals and helped spin and sew. She was very religious. After receiving her first vision at age twelve, Joan pondered what it meant.

When she was seventeen, heavenly voices told her to save France. Joan knew English invaders had taken possession of a large portion of her country. She went to see the commander of the French troops, explaining that God had sent her to free France and to crown the young French *dauphin*, or prince, as the true king. The commander ignored her, but when Joan's prediction that he would lose the next battle came true, he relented.

Joan was given a military escort to see Prince Charles. When she picked him out of a crowd of courtiers and privately revealed to him what prayer he'd asked of God, Charles gave her a fine horse and armor. With Joan as their leader, the French won the battle of Orléans and others too. Although wounded, Joan occupied a seat of honor at the coronation when the prince was crowned King Charles VII of France.

Joan was eventually captured by the English and sentenced to death. King Charles did not come to her rescue. At age nineteen, Joan was burned at the stake. She praised God during the horrible ordeal, crying out, "Jesus!" before she died.[40]

Today, Joan is the patron saint and national heroine of France.

JOAN of ARC

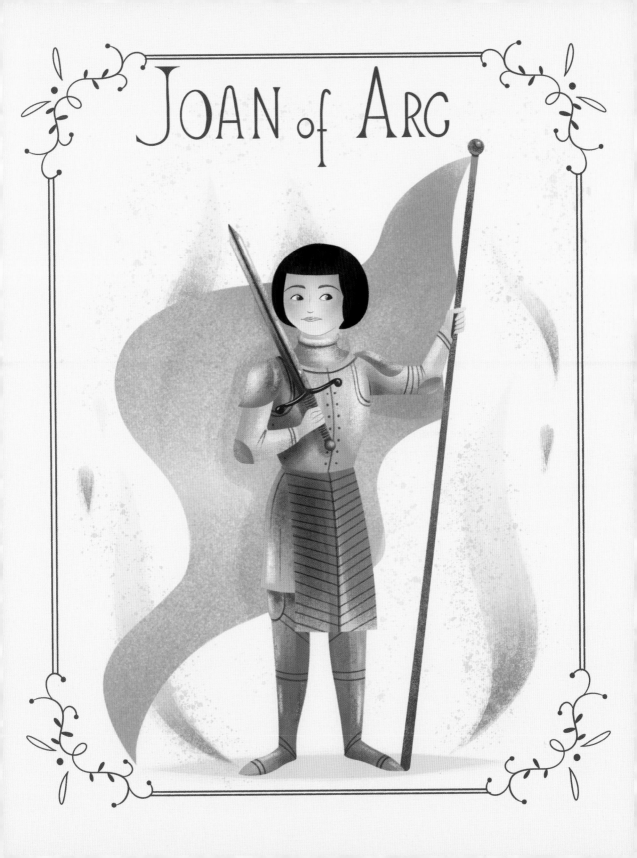

Flannery O'Connor
Faithful Fiction Writer

{ 1925–1964 }

Born in Georgia to devout Catholic parents, Flannery O'Connor was a shy child with a fondness for chickens. She taught one hen to walk backward and even sewed small outfits for her favorite chickens.

She attended Catholic schools and enjoyed drawing cartoons and writing stories. Her father died from lupus when Flannery was sixteen, leaving her devastated with grief.

Flannery attended a nearby women's college and was active in campus life, even serving as the editor of the college's literary magazine. She later attended the University of Iowa, where she earned a master's degree in creative writing.

Deeply religious, Flannery kept a prayer journal, often lamenting how the secular world did not understand people with religious minds and hearts. She also wrote short stories about God and morality.

Flannery became a literary sensation following the publication of her first story, "The Geranium." She quickly earned a reputation as one of the most respected fiction writers of the twentieth century.

After receiving numerous literary honors, Flannery fell ill with lupus, the same incurable disease that killed her father. She returned to her Georgia home to raise peacocks, emus, toucans, and other exotic birds. Even though her health was frail, she continued to write a few hours each day, insisting, "If you have a gift, you have to use it no matter how difficult the circumstances."[41]

Flannery died at the age of thirty-nine in 1964. Eight years later, her collection of short stories earned the National Book Award for Fiction.

Flannery O'Connor

Mary Stone (Shi Meiyu)

China's Little Doctor

{ 1873–1954 }

Shi Meiyu's father, a Methodist pastor, was one of the earliest Chinese converts to Christianity. Her mother served as principal of a Christian school for girls. They raised their daughter without binding her feet. (Rolling girls' toes under their feet and binding them tightly with cloth was a cruel fashion trend intended to make their feet as small as possible. It caused foot ulcers and infections. Girls grew up hobbling on feet smaller than their fists.)

At age nineteen, Meiyu attended the University of Michigan, where she changed her name to Mary Stone. Mary and her friend Ida Kahn became the first Chinese women to be American-trained medical doctors. After graduating with honors, they returned to China to open a hospital for women and children—the first of its kind in that country. They also established China's first nursing school, where Mary supported "natural feet" for girls.

Known affectionately as the "Little Doctor," Mary also preached the gospel. She rejoiced when her patients turned to Christ, the Great Physician, and were healed spiritually as well as physically. As the first president of the Women's Christian Temperance Union in China, Mary campaigned against the use of alcohol, opium, and cigarettes.

During the violent Boxer Rebellion in 1900, Mary fled to Japan. When she returned to China, she opened a larger hospital. One of the regents at the University of Michigan was so impressed with Mary's medical work that he endowed a scholarship for Asian women wishing to study medicine at the university. The Barbour Scholarship continues to provide tuition for female students today.

Wilma Rudolph
Track Star

{ 1940–1994 }

Wilma Rudolph was one of the fastest female runners in the world. When she was a baby in Tennessee, no one predicted she would win three Olympic gold medals, because she was crippled with polio. Wilma even wore a heavy brace on her left leg. Doctors told her mother that Wilma would never be able to walk normally.

But Mrs. Rudolph didn't listen to them. She had faith that God would heal her daughter. She took Wilma to church every Sunday and held family devotions each evening. She frequently drove Wilma to the hospital for physical therapy.

Wilma worked hard. Soon she was walking and then running with amazing speed. When she was fifteen years old, Wilma qualified for the US Olympic track and field team. She traveled to Melbourne, Australia, to participate in the 1956 Olympic Games, where she won a bronze medal in the 400-meter relay.

The world praised her fine athletic performance, but Wilma struggled with disappointment. She felt she'd let her team down because she hadn't won a gold medal. Wilma made up her mind to try harder and asked God for his guidance.

In 1960, she was in top physical condition for the Olympics in Rome. Wilma didn't ask God to let her win the races. She simply prayed he would help her do her best, and he did—Wilma won three gold medals.

Wilma once said, "A Christian athlete is not a person who practices Christianity only on the track or playing field…God goes with me wherever I go."[42]

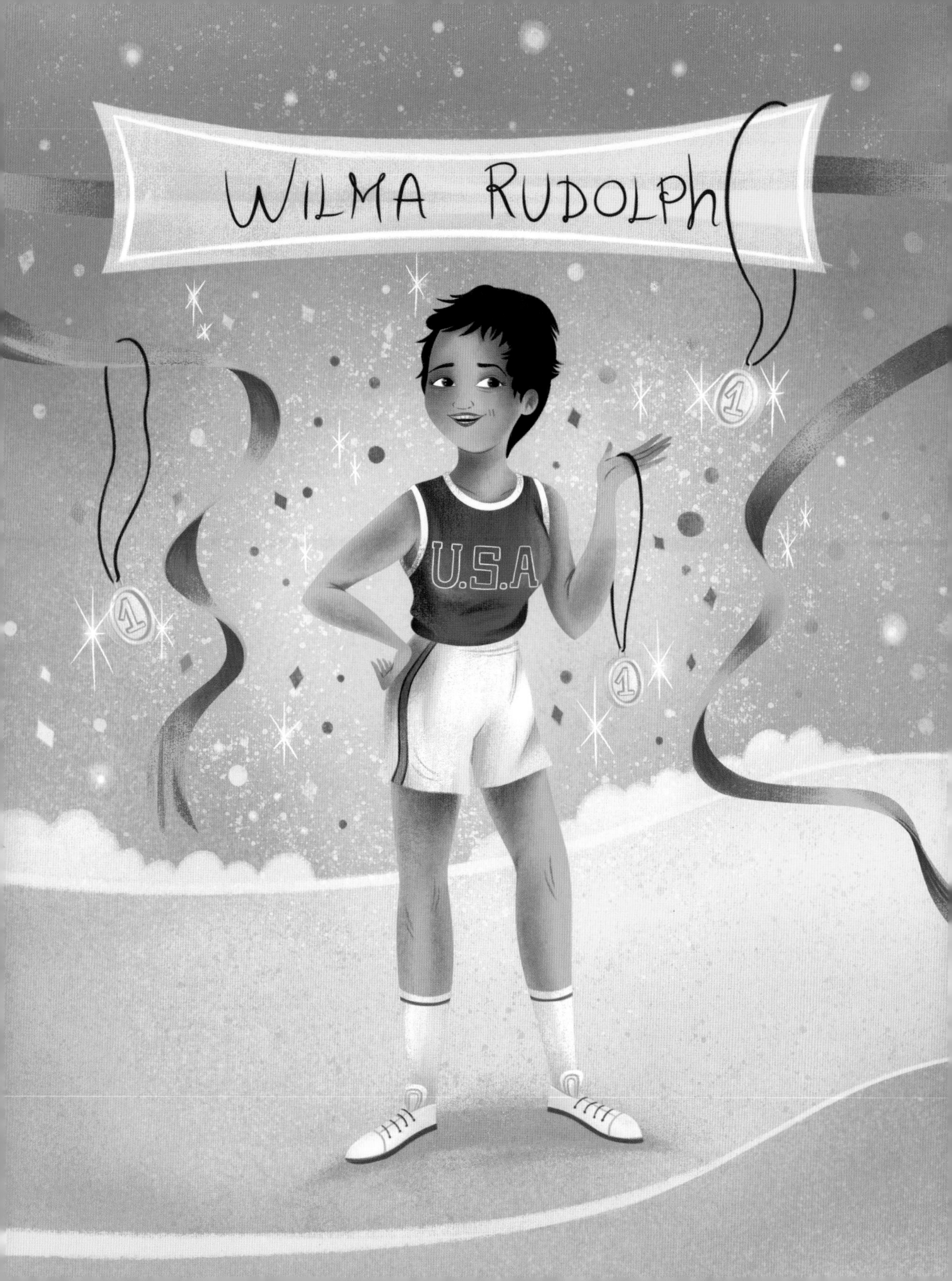
WILMA RUDOLPH
U.S.A
1
1
1

Elisabeth Elliot
Evangelist to Ecuador

{ 1926–2015 }

Brave and adventurous, Elisabeth Howard was only twelve when she prayed, "Lord, I want you to do anything you want with me."[43] She attended Wheaton College, where she studied classical Greek, hoping to translate the New Testament for unreached people groups. She married Jim Elliot in 1953. They joined four other families on the mission field in Ecuador.

While living with the peaceful Quecha tribe, Jim attempted to make contact with the Waorani—a violent tribe known for their revenge killings. Neighboring tribes called them *Aucas*, or savages. When Jim and four others were killed, Elisabeth insisted, "This is not a tragedy. God has a plan and purpose in all this."

Together with Rachel Saint, the sister of one of the other murdered missionaries, Elisabeth took her toddler Valerie to the Waorani village, where they lived for two years in a tiny rainswept hut, eating roasted monkey limbs and other local fare. She hoped that by forgiving those who had killed her husband, she might teach them about God's mercy and grace. Her courageous faith won several in the tribe to faith in Christ and inspired millions of Christians around the world. When Elisabeth returned to the United States in 1963, the Waorani were no longer a violent culture.

Elisabeth married again and began her speaking ministry across the United States. She also wrote twenty-four books, many of them inspirational bestsellers. Today, the tribe she evangelized continues to grow in the Christian faith.

Elisabeth Elliot

Corazon Aquino
Mother of Asian Democracy

{ 1933–2009 }

In 1986, Maria Corazon Aquino became the first female president of the Philippines, restoring democracy after a corrupt dictator fled the country.

Cory, as her friends called her, had never planned for a political career. Shy and religious, she was born into a wealthy banking family. She attended an exclusive Catholic school in Manila. When she was a teenager, her parents sent her to the United States, where she completed college degrees in French and mathematics.

Upon her return to the Philippines, Cory met Benigo Aquino, Jr. They married and had five children. Cory felt content to be a mother and homemaker.

But that was not to be.

Cory's husband spoke out against the brutal policies of Ferdinand Marcos, who'd taken over the country in 1972. Soldiers assassinated Benigo in full view of television cameras, spurring outrage in the Philippines and around the world. With pressure from the United States, Marcos was forced to hold an election.

Urged to run for president, Cory turned to prayer and guidance from her church. The popular widow won the election and quickly began restoring democracy, releasing political prisoners, and repealing repressive labor laws.

Although Marcos supporters tried to have her killed, Cory put her faith in Christ, saying, "I would rather die a meaningful death than live a meaningless life."[44]

After serving as president for six years, Cory refused to run for reelection. However, she remained active in politics for the remainder of her life.

Katharina von Bora
Mother of the Reformation

{ 1499–1552 }

Katharina von Bora was the daughter of a German nobleman. He sent her to monasteries to be educated, encouraging her to become a nun at sixteen. Kate was very bright and took a keen interest in the reforms taking place in the church. She became unhappy with monastic life and longed to leave. However, abandoning one's religious vows often led to scandal and even imprisonment.

Undaunted, Kate and several of her sister nuns wrote a letter to pastor Martin Luther in 1523, asking for help. Luther devised a daring plan, helping the nuns make their escape hidden in a fish merchant's wagon.

None of their families welcomed their return, so the women turned to Luther to help them find respectable husbands. Kate refused to marry anyone but Luther or his closest friend. Despite the fourteen-year difference in their ages, Kate and Martin enjoyed a happy marriage. They lived in a former monastery called the Black Cloister, which was often filled with guests and paying boarders. The couple had six children of their own and adopted four orphans.

Kate proved energetically resourceful in managing the large estate. She enjoyed lively discussions about religion with her dinner guests, earning the nickname "Mother of the Reformation."

Some years after Luther's death, Kate fled her home during a plague outbreak. She died after being injured in a fatal cart accident. Faithful and tenacious to the end, Katharina declared on her deathbed, "I will stick to Christ like a burr to a topcoat."[45]

Sojourner Truth
Social Activist

{ 1797–1883 }

Isabella Baumfree was born a slave in New York. She had several masters as a child, some of them cruel. At age thirty, she had a vision leading her to the home of a Quaker couple who purchased her to set her free.

She later worked as a housekeeper for a Christian evangelist, converted to the Christian faith, and changed her name. She chose "Sojourner" because God told her she would be traveling throughout the land, and she chose "Truth" because that's what she would declare to the people. She felt immense happiness in her faith and testified, "Jesus loved me. I knowed it. I felt it."[46]

She spoke against slavery at churches throughout New England. Because she couldn't read or write, Sojourner dictated her life story to her friend Olive Gilbert in 1850. She delivered her most controversial speech, "Ain't I a Woman?" in 1851 at the Women's Rights Convention in Akron, Ohio, chastising white abolitionists for not seeking civil rights for African-American women as well as men.

But with fame came danger too. A mob attacked her so viciously that Sojourner was forced to use a cane for the remainder of her life. On another occasion, a racist streetcar conductor broke her arm.

After the Civil War, Sojourner petitioned the government to allow freed slaves to purchase land in the West. She worked tirelessly for racial equality until she retired at age 85.

Sojourner Truth

Notes

1 Helen S. Syer, *Pandita Ramabai: The Story of Her Life* (Sun City Center, FL: Revival Press, 2014), 4.

2 Debbie McDaniel, "40 Powerful Quotes from Corrie ten Boom," Crosswalk, May 21, 2015, https://www.crosswalk .com/faith/spiritual-life/inspiring-quotes/40-powerful -quotes-from-corrie-ten-boom.html.

3 Robert Eric Frykenberg, "Setting the Captives Free," *Christian History & Biography*, Spring 2007, issue 94, page 18.

4 Mission Aviation Fellowship, "Betty Greene," https://www.maf.org/about/history/betty-greene.

5 Ashley Andrews, "Ruby Bridges Shares the Key to Overcoming Racism," CBN, https://www1.cbn.com /ruby-bridges-shares-key-overcoming-racism.

6 Tim Ellsworth and Diana Chandler, "U.S. Gold Medalist Gabby Douglas: Glory Goes to God," Baptist Press, August 7, 2012, http://www.bpnews.net/38440 /us-gold-medalist-gabby-douglas-glory-goes-to-god.

7 Pamela Rose Williams, "21 Top Amy Carmichael Quotes," What Christians Want to Know, https://www.whatchristianswanttoknow.com /21-top-amy-carmichael-quotes/.

8 Richard Wurmbrand, *Tortured for Christ, 50ᵗʰ Anniversary Edition* (Colorado Springs, CO: David C. Cook, 2017), 28.

9 Sabina Wurmbrand, *The Pastor's Wife* (Bartlesville, OK: Living Sacrifice Book Company, 2005), 48.

10 "Harriet Tubman: the Moses of Her People," *Christianity Today*, https://www.christianitytoday.com/history/people /activists/harriet-tubman.html.

11 Hannah Pakula, *The Last Empress* (New York, NY: Simon & Schuster, 2009), cited in the *New York Times* book review, https://www.nytimes.com/2009/11/04/books/excerpt-last -empress.html.

12 Tamika Catchings Smith, *Catch a Star: Shining Through Adversity to Become a Champion* (Grand Rapids, MI: Revell, 2016), 248.

13 Stephanie A. Sarkis, "26 Quotes on Faith," *Psychology Today*, Feb. 6, 2011, https://www.psychologytoday.com/us/blog /here-there-and-everywhere/201102/26-quotes-faith.

14 "Fanny Crosby: Prolific and Blind Hymn Writer," *Christianity Today*, http://www.christianitytoday.com /history/people/poets/fanny-crosby.html.

15 "Saint Catherine of Siena Quotes," *The Catholic Reader*, June 3, 2013, http://thecatholicreader.blogspot.com /2013/06/saint-catherine-of-siena-quotes.html.

16 Jerry Dauost, "Mother Teresa and Dorothy Day: Two Radical Women," GodSpy, March 27, 2008, https:// oldarchive.godspy.com/faith/Mother-Teresa-and-Dorothy -Day-Two-Radical-Women.cfm.htm.

17 Dan Graves, "Josephine Butler Championed Women," Christianity.com, June 2007, https://www.christianity.com /church/church-history/timeline/1901-2000/josephine -butler-championed-women-11630685.html.

18 Eric Metaxes, *Seven Women: And the Secret of their Greatness* (Nashville, TN: Nelson Books, 2015), 161.

19 Prerana Korpe, "Rosa Parks and Civil Disobedience," Newseum, December 1, 2015, http://www.newseum .org/2015/12/01/rosa-parks-and-civil-disobedience/.

20 "Anne Bradstreet: America's First Poet," *Christianity Today*, https://www.christianitytoday.com/history/people/poets /anne-bradstreet.html.

21 "Bethany Hamilton," Homeschooling Teen, April 4, 2011, http://homeschoolingteen.com/2011/04/bethany-hamilton/.

22 Antioch Community Church, "Post-session Interview with Christine Caine," September 25, 2013, https://antiochwaco .com/tag/christine-caine/.

23 Jamie Janosz, "Amanda Berry Smith: Turning Obstacles into Gospel Opportunities," *True Woman* (blog), February 11, 2016, https://www.reviveourhearts.com/true-woman/blog /amanda-berry-smith-turning-obstacles-gospel-opport/.

24 Michael G. Hayken, "The Christian Faith of Jane Austen," Crossway, July 29, 2016, https://www.crossway.org/articles /the-christian-faith-of-jane-austen/.

25 Frances Doyle, "Jeanette Li," Biographical Dictionary of Chinese Christianity, http://bdcconline.net/en/stories /li-jeanette.

26 "Harriet Beecher Stowe," *Christianity Today*, https:// www.christianitytoday.com/history/people/ musiciansartistsandwriters/harriet-beecher-stowe.html.

27 Emma Ward, "Perceptive and Personal Quotes by Harriet Beecher Stowe," Literary Ladies Guide, September 23, 2017, https://www.literaryladiesguide.com/author-quotes /quotes-harriet-beecher-stowe/.

28 Kelvin D. Crow, "The Lady with the Lamp," *Christian History* 53, no. 16:35.

29 Ruth M. Bancewicz, "Life in a Purposeful Universe?" Science and Belief, August 24, 2017, https://scienceandbelief.org/2017/08/24/life-in-a-purposeful-universe/.

30 "Joni Eareckson Tada Story," http://joniearecksontadastory.com/jonis-story-page-3/.

31 Jackie C. Horne, *Conversations with Madeleine L'Engle* (Jackson, MI: University Press of Mississippi, 2018), 70.

32 "In the Midst of Savage Darkness," PBS, 2001 https://www.pbs.org/weta/thewest/program/episodes/two/savagedark.htm.

33 Mary Louise Clifford and J. Candace Clifford, *Women Who Kept the Lights* (Alexandria, VA: Cypress Communications, 2000), 95.

34 Stoyan Zaimov, "Condoleezza Rice Shares Christian Faith with Students, Advises Them to Trust in the Holy Spirit," The Christian Post, November 15, 2011, https://www.christianpost.com/news/condoleezza-rice-shares-christian-faith-with-students-advises-them-to-trust-in-the-holy-spirit-61896/.

35 "Betty Ann Olsen," The Alliance, https://www.cmalliance.org/about/history/in-the-line-of-fire/olsen.

36 Metaxes, *Seven Women*, 175.

37 Lt. Col. William J. Manning, "Chaplain's Corner: Clara Barton, an American Heroine," May 23, 2013, https://www.army.mil/article/104031/chaplains_corner_clara_barton_an_american_heroine.

38 Chloe Pantazi, "Watch the Heartwarming Moment a 98-Year-Old NASA Mathematician Was Honored at the Oscars," Insider, February 27, 2017, https://www.thisisinsider.com/nasa-mathematician-katherine-johnson-oscars-2017-2.

39 Jewell Johnson, *The Top 100 Women of the Christian Faith* (Uhrichsville, OH: Barbour, 2013), 46.

40 Metaxes, *Seven Women*, 27.

41 Elizabeth Kvernen, "Flannery O'Connor, Fiction Fired by Faith," Collegeville Institute, March 24, 2016, https://collegevilleinstitute.org/bearings/flannery-oconnor-fiction-fired-faith/.

42 "Wilma Rudolph," chap. 18 in Ted Simonson, ed., *The Goal and the Glory* (Christian Classics Ethereal Library, 1990), http://www.ccel.us/goal.ch18.html.

43 Ruth Tucker, *From Jerusalem to Irian Jaya: A Biographical History of Christian Missions* (Grand Rapids, MI: Zondervan, 1983), 318.

44 Jone Johnson Lewis, "Corazon Aquino Quotes," Thoughtco, March 25, 2017, https://www.thoughtco.com/corazon-aquino-quotes-3530055.

45 Kristin Tabb, "The Runaway Nun," Desiring God, October 30, 2017, https://www.desiringgod.org/articles/the-runaway-nun.

46 "Sojourner Truth," *Christianity Today*, http://www.christianitytoday.com/history/people/activists/sojourner-truth.html.

About the Author

Shirley Raye Redmond is an award-winning writer and newspaper columnist. Her book *Patriots in Petticoats: Heroines of the American Revolution* was named one of the best children's books of 2004 by the Bank Street College of Education in New York. She is also a part-time instructor for the Institute of Children's Literature, a sought-after workshop speaker, and a member of the Society of Children's Book Writers and Illustrators.

About the Artist

Katya Longhi was born in a small town in southern Italy and studied at the Art Academy in Florence and the Nemo NT Academy of Digital Arts. In her spare time, Katya loves to read fairy tales and collect snow globes. She currently works as a freelance illustrator based in Vercelli and has shown her art in numerous exhibitions throughout Italy.

BE A Courageous WORLD CHANGER!

The 50 fearless heroes
featured in this book
aren't the only ones
who changed the world.

Read about the inspiring lives of more champions of the faith at
courageousworldchangers.com.

SOJOURNER TRUTH · MADELEINE L'ENGLE
POCAHONTAS · ELIZABETH BLACKWELL
WILMA RUDOLPH · KATHARINA von BORA
NARCISSA WHITMAN · ELISABETH ELLIOT
KATHERINE G. JOHNSON · JEANETTE LI
JOAN of ARC · FLANNERY O'CONNOR
CLARA BARTON · SUSAN B. ANTHONY
JONI EARECKSON TADA · NANCY PEARCEY
CONDOLEEZZA RICE · MOTHER TERESA
BETTY OLSEN · HARRIET BEECHER STOWE
FLORENCE NIGHTINGALE · JANE AUSTEN
CORAZON AQUINO · JENNIFER WISEMAN
MARY STONE (SHI MEIYU) · IDA LEWIS

PANDITA RAMABAI · CHRISTINE CAINE
ROSA PARKS · BETHANY HAMILTON
RUBY BRIDGES HALL · HANNAH
MORE · GABRIELLE "GABBY" DOUGLAS
AMANDA SMITH · HARRIET ROSS TUBMAN
MAHALIA JACKSON · AMY CARMICHAEL
NI KWEI-TSENG SOONG · LYDIA DARRAGH
SABINA WURMBRAND · DOROTHY DAY
CORNELIA "CORRIE" TEN BOOM · PHILLIS
WHEATLEY · TAMIKA CATCHINGS SMITH
JOSEPHINE BUTLER · CATHERINE BOOTH
ANNE BRADSTREET · ELIZABETH GREEN
CATHERINE OF SIENA · FANNY CROSBY